Jaguar
XK8 and X

1995 to 2008

ISBN 1 84155 211 9
13-ISBN 978-1-84155-211-8

www.cppress.co.uk

Text and photography by Colin Pitt

Contents

First Generation
Jaguar XK8 Coupe
Production Figures

Date	Quantity
1995	8
1996	2925
1997	5141
1998	3319
1999	1701
2000	1514
2001	1723
2002	1203
2003	985
2004	627
2005	602
Total	19748 Cars

First Generation
Jaguar XKR Coupe
Production Figures

Date	Seconds
1997	11
1998	1402
1999	1530
2000	1778
2001	1659
2002	1053
2003	936
2004	708
2005	584
Total	9661 Cars

First Generation
Jaguar XK8 Convertible

Production Figures

Date	Quantity
1995	12
1996	4187
1997	9765
1998	7662
1999	6196
2000	5907
2001	4404
2002	2910
2003	2280
2004	2003
2005	1434
Total	46 760 Cars

First Generation
Jaguar XKR Convertible

Production Figures

Date	Seconds
1997	12
1998	838
1999	1994
2000	3042
2001	2949
2002	1695
2003	1455
2004	1075
2005	835
Total	13 895 Cars

First Generation
Jaguar XK8

Specifications

XKR Coupe Cost	£59,300
XKR Convertible Cost	£66,300
Engine Cylinders	8
Valves Per Cylinder	4
Bore and Stroke	86mm x 86mm
Capacity	3,996 cc
Maximum Power	370 bhp @ 6150 rpm
Maximum Torque	387 lb/ft @ 3600 rpm
Top Speed	155 mph
Kerb Weight	1640 (coupe)
	1750 (convertible)
Economy Urban	15.7 mpg
Economy Extra Urban	30.0 mpg
Economy Combined	22.5 mpg

Jaguar XK8

The Jaguar XK8, seen here in Sloane Square

Jaguar XK8

Jaguar XK8

Acceleration From Rest		Acceleration In Kickdown	
MPH	Seconds	MPH	Seconds
30	2.3	10-30	2.1
40	3.4	20-40	2.2
50	4.9	30-50	2.6
60	6.6	40-60	3.2
70	8.4	50-70	3.5
80	10.7	60-80	4.1
90	13.5	70-90	5.1
100	16.7	8--100	6.0

Jaguar XK8

The Jaguar XK8 can achieve 0-30 mph in 2.3 seconds and 0-70 mph in 8.4 seconds
Tyres fitted are Pirelli P-Zero 245/50 ZR 17s
Below can be seen one of the last old shape Jaguar XK8s, in Chelsea

Jaguar XK8 Convertible

Jaguar XK8 Convertible, seen here in High Street Kensington

Jaguar XK8 Convertible

This is an earlier Jaguar XK8 Convertible from 1996

Jaguar XK8 Convertible

A Jaguar XKR Convertible, this is a 2000 model

Jaguar XK8 Convertible

The Jaguar XKR Convertible is seen here in Sloane Square

Jaguar XK8 Convertible

The Jaguar XKR Convertible is seen here in Brentwood

Jaguar XK8 Convertible

The "old shape" Jaguar XKR Convertible

Jaguar XKR

Engine

8 Cylinder 3996 cc

Maximum Power:	370 bhp @ 6100 rpm
Maximum Torque:	387 lb @ 3600 rpm
Power to weight:	214 bhp per tonne

Gearbox

Ratios/mph per 1000 rpm

1st	3.59/7.3
2nd	2.19/12.0
3rd	1.41/18.6
4th	1.00/26.3
5th	0.83/31.7

Final Drive 3.06

Acceleration from Rest

0-30 mph	2.2 seconds
0-50 mph	4.2 seconds
0-70 mph	6.9 seconds
0-80 mph	8.9 seconds

Jaguar XKR Convertible

Above is seen the interior of the Jaguar XKR Convertible and below, the XKR badge

Jaguar XKR Convertible

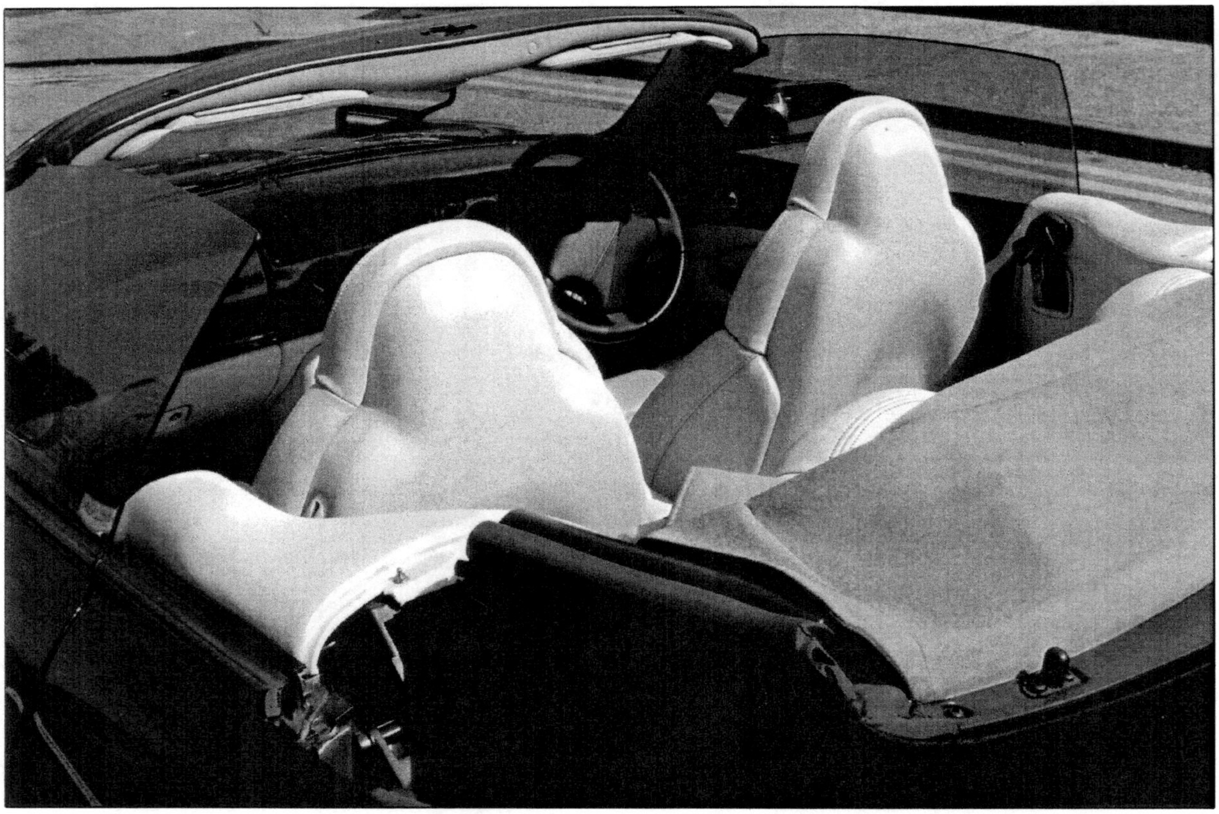

Interior of the Jaguar XKR with the roof down

Jaguar XKR Convertible

The "old shape" Jaguar XKR, seen here in Rayleigh, Essex.
This is one of the last of this shape.

Jaguar XKR Convertible

This particular Jaguar XKR Convertible has a very expensive number plate – R35.

Jaguar XKR Convertible

The "old shape" Jaguar XKR convertible is seen here in Sloane Square.

Jaguar XK8 Vs Bently Continental T

	Jaguar XK8	Bentley Continental T
Capacity	3996cc	6750cc
Power bhp/rpm	284/6100	400/4000
Torque lb ft/rpm	277/4250	590/2000
0-60 mph	6.5 seconds	5.8 seconds
Maximum Speed	156 mph	155 mph
Price New	£47,950	£220,312

Jaguar XKR Vs Maserati 3200 GT

	Jaguar XKR	Maserati 3200 GT
Price New	£60,010	£60,765
0-60 mph	5.1 seconds	5.0 seconds
0-100mph	12.4 seconds	12.7 seconds
30-70 mph (through gears)	4.4 seconds	4.3 seconds
Top Speed	155 mph	164 mph

Maximum Power	370 bhp @ 6150 rpm	370 bhp @ 6250 rpm
Maximum Torque	387 lb ft @ 3600 rpm	362 lb ft @4500 rpm
Bore and Stroke	86mm by 86mm	80mm by 80mm

Gearbox Ratios (Ratios/mph per 1000 rpm)		
1st	3.59/7.3	4.23/5.5
2nd	2.19/12.0	2.51/9.3
3rd	1.41/18.6	1.67/13.9
4th	1.00/26.3	1.23/19.0
5th	0.83/31.7	1.00/23.3
Final Drive Ratio	3.06	3.23

Jaguar XK8

The new shape Jaguar XK8 seen here in the Temple.

Jaguar XK8

The new shape Jaguar XK8 is seen here in High Street Kensington.

Jaguar XK8

The interior of the new shape Jaguar XK8

Jaguar XK8

The Jaguar XK8 seen here near the Royal Albert Hall, South Kensington

Jaguar XK8

The Jaguar XK8 Convertible seen here in Chelsea

Jaguar XK8

The Jaguar XK8 Convertible seen here in Sloane Square, London

Jaguar XK8

The Jaguar XK8 Convertible with the number plate '9 0S' seen here in South Kensington

Jaguar XK8

An Early Jaguar XK8 seen here in Central London

Jaguar XKR

The Jaguar XKR Convertible seen here in Chelsea

Jaguar XKR

The Jaguar XKR Convertible seen here in Emerson Park, Hornchurch

Jaguar XKR

Above, a Jaguar XK8 in Chelsea, and below a Jaguar XKR Convertible seen in Rutland Court, South Kensington

Jaguar XK8

Jaguar XK8's seen in Knightsbridge

Jaguar XK8

Above, a Jaguar XK8 Convertible seen in Knightsbridge, and below a Jaguar XK8 Convertible seen outside the Vitoria and Albert Museum

Jaguar XK 4.2

The new shape Jaguar XK 4.2 Convertible seen here in Sloane Square, London

Jaguar XK 4.2

The new shape Jaguar XK 4.2 seen here in High Street Kensington

Jaguar XK 4.2

New shape Jaguar XK 4.2 with the distinctive number plate '90 AZ'

Jaguar XK 4.2

New shape Jaguar XK 4.2 seen here outside a hotel in Earl's Court, London

Jaguar XK 4.2

The new shape Jaguar XK 4.2 seen here in Temple, London

Jaguar XK 4.2

The latest shape Jaguar XK 4.2 Convertible with the distinctive registration number '61 TR' seen here in Emerson Park, Hornchurch

Jaguar XK 4.2

Latest shape Jaguar XK 4.2 Convertible seen outside Jaguar Main Agent's in Mayfair, London

Jaguar XK 4.2

Latest shape Jaguar XK 4.2 seen here in South Kensington, London

Jaguar XK 4.2

The new shape Jaguar XK 4.2 seen here in Chelsea

No 4774 AUTOCAR ROAD TEST

Jaguar XKR

For Image, effortless pace, muscular engine, body control
Against Interior details, unsupportive seats, small fuel tank

PHOTOGRAPHY STAN PAPIOR

QUICK FACTS

Model tested	XKR
Price	£67,495
On sale	Now
0-60mph	5.2sec
Top speed	155mph (limited)
70-0mph	46.7m
Skidpan	0.92g
Economy	19.1mpg
CO_2 emissions	294g/km

Since its introduction in 1998, the XKR has been Jaguar's flagship, mating supercharged V8 power with its most sensuous of coupé and convertible bodies. Following the widely acclaimed launch of the new XK – road tested in the 3 May issue – the Coventry-based company is bullish about its new supercharged sports car. It uses the same basic ingredients as the regular car – aluminium construction with a riveted and bonded joining method, rear-drive V8 power and an automatic gearbox – but adds a dash of aggression to the styling and the promise of a more keenly focused driving experience.

Most of all, the XKR has the potential to address the one major criticism we had of the new XK: a lack of poke. It wasn't that we expected the naturally aspirated XK to be a leather-lined dragster, just that a luxury sports GT should accelerate across the landscape with demure authority, and there were times when the rather uncouth V8 – only lightly fettled from the old XK8 – seemed to be making a meal of it. In short, it appeared as if Jaguar, forced to count pennies carefully, had spent the money on the advanced aluminium chassis rather than in the engine room.

Not that the engine in the supercharged XKR appears to be much changed from the previous XKR, either. There's now an extra 20bhp, taking the peak power to 420bhp, and a slight increase in torque to 413lb ft. Most of these gains are achieved through new twin air inlets and a variable timing system fitted to the inlet cams of the 90-degree V8. Overall engine capacity stays at 4196cc, with an Eaton-type supercharger continuing to provide the forced induction into the cylinders. But, as with the XK, the XKR proved disappointing on our scales, despite its aluminium construction. Weighing in at 1780kg (with options), our test car was 100kg heavier than Jaguar's claim.

It takes a keen eye to spot an XKR, but the differences are there. The frontal area is considerably more aggressive, with deeper mesh grilles and separate mesh-filled side intakes. The bonnet also features slightly crass air intakes embossed with the word 'supercharged'. On the flanks, the side strakes are now alloy-effect plastic, while a quartet of no-nonsense tailpipes exits at the rear of the car. Overall, it's a successful tone-up.

Depress the red start button and the XKR kicks into life with a determined growl. Unlike the semi-active exhaust system on the standard XK that relies on back pressure to silence noise when cruising, the system on the XK is fully active. The car's ECU controls the silencers, dampening exhaust noise when cruising, but opening the tubes to full volume when you're going for it.

Even after just a few miles, the worth of that extra muscle is abundantly clear. Now, you only have to make partial use of the accelerator and the big cat surges past other traffic with ease, making it a more relaxed car than the standard model during everyday driving. There's less supercharger whine than in the old car – a deliberately engineered change – and when you start to really use the performance, there's a delicious, diamond-hard cackle from the exhausts above 4000rpm. There's bite with this bark too; although we failed to match Jaguar's acceleration claims (our test car had an electronics glitch that prevented us from fully disabling the traction →

VU06 RZP

JAGUAR XKR DATA

WHAT IT COSTS

On-the-road price	£67,495
Price as tested	£71,862
Retained value 3yrs	na
Typical PCP pcm	na
Contract hire pcm	na
Cost per mile	na
CO_2	294g/km
Tax at 22/40% pcm	£431/£984
Insurance/typical quote	20/£809

EQUIPMENT CHECK LIST

20in alloy wheels	**£2500**
Active lights	**£430**
Cruise control	**£995**
Keyless entry	**£430**

Options in **bold** fitted to test car
■ = Standard na = not available

Front track 1560mm **Rear track** 1608mm **Width including mirrors** 2080mm
Width excluding mirrors 1892mm **Front interior width** 1430mm **Boot space** 300 litres

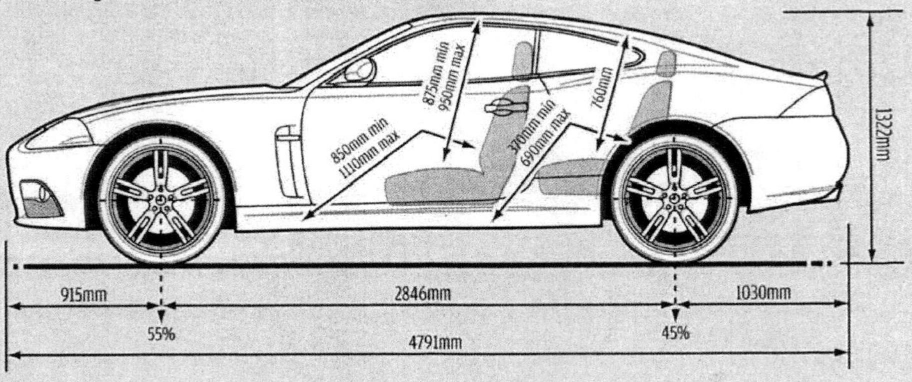

SPECIFICATIONS

ENGINE

Type	V8, supercharged, 4196cc
Made of	Alloy head and block
Installation	Front, longitudinal, rwd
Power	420bhp at 6250rpm
Torque	413lb ft at 4000rpm
Red line	6250rpm
Power to weight	246bhp per tonne
Torque to weight	248lb ft per tonne
Specific output	98bhp per litre
Bore/stroke	86.0/90.3mm
Compression ratio	9.1:1
Valve gear	4 per cyl, dohc
Fuel type	Unleaded

CHASSIS & BODY

Construction	Aluminium monocoque
Weight	1665kg
Weight as tested	1780kg
Drag coefficient	0.34Cd
Wheels	20in
Made of	Alloy
Tyres F/R	255/35 ZR20, 285/30 ZR20 Dunlop SP Sport Maxx
Spare	Spacesaver

TRANSMISSION

Type Rear-wheel drive
Gearbox 6-speed automatic
Ratios/mph per 1000rpm
1st 4.171/5.8 **2nd** 2.34/10.3 **3rd** 1.521/15.8
4th 1.143/21.0 **5th** 0.691/27.7 **6th** 0.691/34.8
Final drive ratio 3.31/7.26

SUSPENSION

Front Double wishbones, coil springs, anti-roll bar, electronic dampers
Rear Five-link, coil springs, anti-roll bar, electronic dampers

STEERING

Type Electronic power assistance
Turns lock to lock 2.7
Turning circle 11.0m

To read our TOP 100 ROAD TESTS go to autocar.co.uk

BRAKES

Front 355mm ventilated discs
Rear 326mm ventilated discs
Anti-lock Standard, with brake assist
Parking brake Electronically operated

SAFETY

Driver, passenger, side and head airbags, ESP, traction control

Road test results Dry, sunny, 18C. Odometer reading 4627 miles

ACCELERATION

Standing qtr mile 13.7sec/107.4mph **Standing km** 24.4sec/136.5mph **30-70mph** 4.3sec

30mph	40	50	60	70	80	90	100	110	120	130	140
2.2s	3.1s	4.1s	5.2s	6.6s	8.1s	9.8s	11.8s	14.4s	17.1s	20.6s	26.0s

BRAKING

60-0mph 2.9sec **Indicated mph at 30/70** 32/74mph

30mph-0	50mph-0	70mph-0
8.9m	23.9m	46.7m

POWER & TORQUE

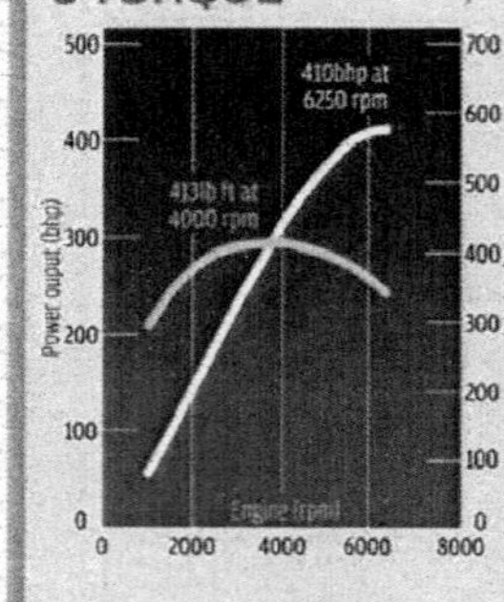

ACCELERATION IN GEAR

	Kickdown
20-40	1.6
30-50	1.9
40-60	2.1
50-70	2.5
60-80	3.0
70-90	3.2
90-110	4.6

MAX SPEEDS IN GEAR

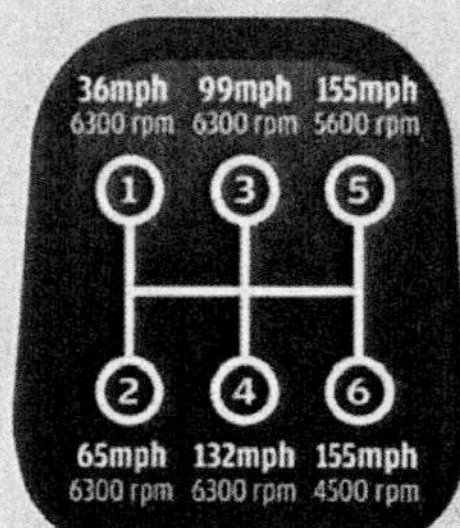

HANDLING

Lateral acceleration	0.92*g*
Balance	Neutral to oversteer
Seat support	Average

ECONOMY

TEST	**Average**	19.1mpg
	Touring	23.9mpg
	Track	9.2mpg
CLAIMED	**Urban**	14.8mpg
	Extra-urban	32.9mpg
	Combined	22.9mpg

Tank size 71 litres **Test range** 373 miles

CABIN NOISE

Idle 49dbA **Max revs in third gear** 76dbA
30mph 61dbA **50mph** 64dbA **70mph** 69dbA

HEADLIGHTS

Dipped beam Good
Full beam Good
Test notes Fine range and brightness

THE SMALL PRINT *Power-to-weight and torque-to-weight figures calculated using manufacturer's claimed kerbweight. For information on the Jaguar XKR, contact Jaguar Cars Limited, Browns lane, Allesley, Coventry CV5 9DR (0800 70 80 60) www.jaguar.co.uk. Cost-per-mile figures calculated over three years/36,000 miles, including depreciation and maintenance but not insurance; Lloyds TSB Autolease (0870 600 6333). Insurance quote covers 35-year-old professional male with clean licence and full no-claims bonus living in Swindon; from What Car? Insurance (0845 123 2618). Contract hire figure based on a three-year lease/36,000-mile contract including maintenance; from Lombard (0870 902 3311).

PETER LIDDIARD

Cabin design a vast improvement over the old XKR but still not special enough

Boot space is adequate and no more

Rear seat space severely restricted

QUICK COMPARISON
Smooth operator versus extreme sport

Jaguar XKR
Price £67,495
On sale in the UK now
0-60mph 5.2sec
Economy 22.9mpg (claimed)

Porsche 911 Carrera S
Price £65,860
On sale in the UK now
0-60mph 4.6sec
Economy 24.6mpg (claimed)

COULD THESE two possibly be more different? One is an enduring classic, seen by some as an engineering relic way past its sell-by date, but considered by others to be the greatest sports car of all time. The other is as conventional as a grand tourer can get and carries a considerable weight of expectation. It needs to succeed for the sake of its maker's long-term health.

You sit low, but strangely upright in the 911. Despite its metamorphosis into a 'modern' car in 1998, the windscreen still seems close and upright, and the driving environment still uniquely Porsche. You could call it dour inside, but the overall quality feels good. Turn the key and the flat six churns into life with a characteristic splutter. Its manual gearbox boasts perhaps the best gearshift quality in the world, and every control shares a beautiful consistency of weighting. The 911's 350bhp might not sound like a great deal by today's standards, but when it's a powerplant of this quality – great mid-range punch, extraordinary smoothness – bald power figures don't matter. Driving it is still an acquired taste, though, with plenty of front-end bob over bumpy roads and that typical 911 rear bias.

There's much more room in the back of the Porsche than the Jag, and its size makes it easier to thread in and out of traffic. Where it loses out is in ride comfort. The Jag shames the German for road and wind noise, too. Considering they're both performance cars priced at remarkably similar levels, you couldn't get two more different ways of spending your cash.

The Porsche 911: same price as the Jag, but it couldn't be more different

← control) there's no doubting the storming pace on offer here. The 30-70mph sprint, for example, vanishes in just 4.3sec. High-speed cruising is a forté, too, with effortless punch at high speeds (the 90-110mph increment takes just 4.6sec) before the XKR is eventually reined in by an electronic limiter at 155mph. Even so, if we were being really picky, the blown AJ-V8 lacks the syrupy-smooth sweetness of a Maserati V8, or the big-lung punch of the new AMG 6.2-litre V8.

However, the gearbox is superb. The shift programs have been massaged for the XKR and whether you're driving normally – where the added torque has helped the 'box become more decisive – or enjoying the blipped downshifts in manual mode, it's hard to fault. Larger brakes, now 355mm at the front, complete a compelling package.

To make the XKR a sharper driver's tool, Jaguar has uprated the springs – they're now 38 per cent stiffer at the front and 24 per cent stiffer at the rear – and retuned the CATS adaptive dampers. The steering has also been fettled both mechanically and electronically via the servotronic power steering maps. To fully understand the XKR, though, you need to appreciate Jaguar's intentions: namely, to create a sporting GT that doesn't sacrifice comfort and everyday usability. Therefore, don't expect the wild but intimate connection of man and machine found inside a Maserati GranSport. Instead, the Jag is a subtle but purposeful evolution of the regular XK, shifting its abilities further towards the driver-orientated end of the market without harming its talent to waft. Apart from a low-speed ride that's mildly hobbled by the fitting of spectacular, optional 20-inch wheels, the XKR is cosseting and comfortable over a variety of road surfaces. As the speeds rise, it never fights the road, choosing instead to work with the contours of the asphalt in what Jaguar's engineers call 'breathing'. It's a trait shared by all the current Jaguars, and a mightily effective one on our pockmarked roads. Grip levels are superb, and even without a limited-slip differential the XKR will indulge in a dose of power oversteer. It's only the steering that still slightly disappoints. Yes, it's a better instrument for fast driving than the regular car's rack, but for us there's still too much dead feeling around the straight-ahead. While you're in this trough, it's too easily affected by bumps in the road and a faux self-centring action. It's a pity because, once you're turned in, it's nicely weighted with good feedback, despite the occasional kickback over the worst potholes.

Inside, the XKR is very similar to its lesser brethren. This means a monumental improvement in ergonomics and functionality over the old car, but also a cabin that's simply not special enough for a car costing £70k. The odd logo here and there, a unique alloy trim strip and wide but unsupportive sports seats are not enough. Other flaws remain: the rear seats are next to useless and the boot space stingy, while the 71-litre fuel tank is just enough to provide adequate touring range (we achieved 23.9mpg), but drains quickly if you're pressing on. Nevertheless, at £67,495, the XKR feels like a lot of car for the money.

AUTOCAR VERDICT

This is a superb effort from Jaguar, blending enormous pace with a comfortable vibe that makes it a compelling car either for everyday use, or as an occasional treat. It's not perfect, but it proves Jaguar can make truly world-class cars, a fact that should make enthusiasts everywhere very glad.

Quick, cosseting and effective sports GT ★★★★☆

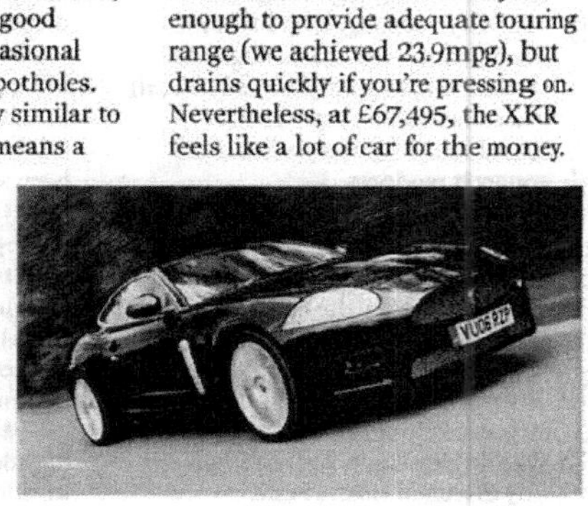

No 4753 AUTOCAR GT ROADTEST

Jaguar XK

Jaguar is promising us a more modern, athletic and inspirational GT with its new XK. Has it delivered?

PHOTOGRAPHY MITCH PESHAVRIA

BF06 DAA

No 4753 AUTOCAR GT ROADTEST

QUICK FACTS

Model tested	Jaguar XK
Price	£58,995
On sale	Now
0-60mph	6.0sec
Top speed	146mph
Economy	21.9mpg
Emissions	269g/km
70-0mph	53.5m
Skidpan	0.83g

For Jaguar enthusiasts, the pairing of the letters 'X' and 'K' has long equalled excitement. Although the mainstay of the Coventry marque's business is rooted in saloons, it is sports cars and coupés that have put Jags on people's most-wanted lists for decades. Almost 60 years ago, Jaguar redefined sports cars with the 1948 XK, clothing a big engine and big performance in bodywork svelte to the point of sensual.

Jaguar has been offering much the same formula ever since, if with the occasional change of emphasis. The XK was succeeded by the legendary E-type, known as the XKE in America. Jaguar's most famous car, it was a sensational looker whose existence has almost become a mill-stone for the company's designers.

The E-type eventually turned fatter and softer, before being succeeded by the fixed-head XJS in 1975. The XJS's combination of coupé bodywork and effortlessly refined power directed Jaguar's sports models towards the grand tourer and away from raw sports cars, a trend continued with the XK8 of 1996.

Now we have the XK. It replaces the XK8 and comes at a critical time for a Jaguar battling to escape red ink, falling sales and uncomfortable questions about its future. The XK is not the car to save the company – it will be produced in too few numbers for that – but if it succeeds it will go some way to restore Ford's much-tested faith in the marque.

With 'only' 295bhp and no limited-slip diff, you have to be brutal to get XK to do this; handling very benign, though

DESIGN & ENGINEERING

Even before the XK arrived on our roads it attracted controversy as a design. We shouldn't be surprised: a cornerstone of a Jaguar's appeal has always been its sensuous styling, and image is more important than ever in these design-savvy times. Although it is for the individual to decide, we can't ignore the groundswell of opinion that gathered during our test. The new XK has presence – from some angles it is strikingly handsome – but it isn't quite the 'gorgeous' vision in aluminium that Jaguar's marketing suits would have us believe.

This is a conservative design, its classical coupé proportions mixed with strong Jaguar hallmarks such as the ovoid intake 'mouth'. Perhaps the biggest change is that the fuselage shape of the XK8's lower body has been traded for a Coke-bottle form that heightens the XK's muscularity, as do shorter overhangs and a wider track.

It is the larger details that split opinions most: the bluff nose, the slightly shapeless headlamps and the round tail-lights provoking most debate. Some believe the overall design should have been more adventurous.

Many will gaze at the XK's bodywork without realising that the metal itself is what sets this new Jaguar apart. Like the XJ, it uses Jaguar's epoxy-bonded and riveted aluminium monocoque construction (see tech box, p33). Not only does this make the XK 30 per cent stiffer than the old XK8, it is also 90kg lighter at a claimed 1595kg.

But Autocar's scales produced a disappointment, our heavily optioned XK weighing in at 1725kg, or 130kg more. That's almost the weight of two passengers. Either the XK has gained pounds in the birthing process, or Jaguar's options carry considerable heft.

Mechanically the XK is less advanced. The engine sits up front and drives the rear wheels, while coil-sprung unequal-length wishbones suspend both axles, the driveshafts doubling as the upper links at the rear. Jaguar's CATS adaptive damping is optional, and upgraded to treat each shock absorber individually as it calculates the ideal damping mode.

It's in the engine room that Jaguar has made the least changes. The AJ-V8 from the XK8 has had only small revisions, the key alteration affecting the fuel injectors, which are now multi-holed for finer spray control. Otherwise the all-alloy 4196cc V8 is unchanged, with its four

Soft chassis set-up gives fine ride at all speeds, if plenty of body roll

cams, variable inlet valve timing and variable camshaft phasing. It puts out 295bhp and 310lb ft of torque – adequate rather than spectacular outputs in the class. Instead, the XK relies on its (theoretical) low weight to compensate.

PERFORMANCE AND DYNAMICS

Those used to sporting Jaguars that can barely be heard at idle will be surprised by the XK – its exhausts have been tuned for rort. At low speeds you hear a distant but insistent chug, closer to that of a Rover V8-powered sports car than the turbine growl of a BMW 650i or Mercedes SL500, and it's a lot louder if you're outside. Yet the XK still serves that languidly powerful progress that has long been a Jaguar trademark. It feels unstressed – as do you – yet has the potency (just) to lunge for gaps in the traffic.

The speed-sensitive steering is finger-light, the general refinement excellent, and the ride – for the →

JAGUAR XK DATA

DIMENSIONS

Front track 1560mm **Rear track** 1598mm **Width including mirrors** 2065mm
Width excluding mirrors 1800mm **Front interior width** 1530mm **Boot volume** 330 litres

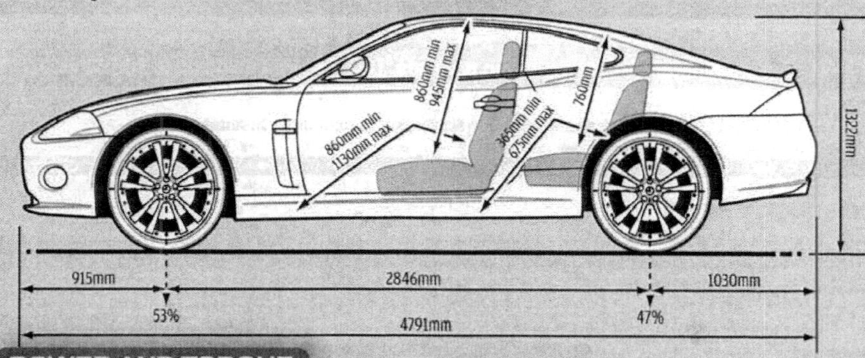

POWER AND TORQUE

ENGINE

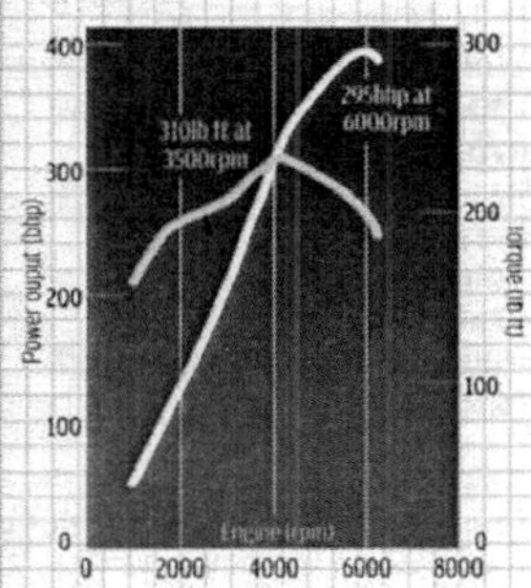

ENGINE VITALS

Red line
6800rpm
Power
295bhp at 6000rpm
Torque
310lb ft at 3500rpm

Type/fuel	V8, 4196cc, petrol
Made of/installation	Alloy/front, longitudinal, rwd
Power/torque to weight	185bhp/194lb ft per tonne
Specific output	70bhp per litre
Comp ratio / bore/stroke	11.0:1 / 86.0/90.3mm
Valve gear	4 per cyl, DOHC

CHASSIS & BODY

Construction	Aluminium monocoque
Weight/as tested	1595kg/1725kg
Drag coefficient	0.33
Wheels	8.5J x 20in/9.5J x 20in, alloy
Tyres	255/35 R20 / 285/30 R20 Dunlop SP Sport Maxx

TRANSMISSION

Gearbox 6-speed automatic
Ratios/mph per 1000rpm Final drive ratio 3.311
1st 4.171/5.8 **2nd** 2.340/10.3 **3rd** 1.521/15.8
4th 1.143/21.0 **5th** 0.867/27.7 **6th** 0.691/34.8

SUSPENSION

Front Double wishbones, coil springs, anti-roll bar, electronic dampers
Rear Wishbone, coil springs, anti-roll bar, electronic dampers

STEERING

Type Electric power assistance
Turns lock-to-lock 2.7 **Turning circle** na

BRAKES

Front 326mm ventilated discs **Rear** 326mm ventilated discs
Anti-lock Standard **Parking brake** Electronically operated

THE SMALL PRINT *Power- and torque-to-weight figures calculated using manufacturer's claimed kerbweight. © Autocar 2006. Test results may not be reproduced without editor's written permission. For information on the Jaguar XK contact Jaguar Cars Limited, Browns Lane, Allesley, Coventry CV5 9DR, 0800 708060, www.jaguar.com. Cost-per-mile figures calculated over three years/36,000 miles, including depreciation and maintenance but not insurance; Lloyds TSB Autolease (0870 600 6333). Insurance quote covers 35-year-old professional male with clean licence and full no-claims bonus living in Swindon; from What Car? Insurance (0845 123 2618). Contract hire figure based on a three-year lease/36,000-mile contract including maintenance; from Lombard (0870 902 3311).

XK has sports car sound, if not pace: 0-60mph in 6.0sec; optional 20in alloys look fantastic; brakes fade too quickly

No 4753 AUTOCAR **GT** ROADTEST

JAGUAR XK *GT DATA*

TRACK Sunshine and showers, damp patches, 10C. Odometer reading 2058 miles

ACCELERATION

Standing qtr mile 14.6sec/99.2mph **Standing km** 26.6sec/123.8mph **30-70mph** 5.3sec

30mph	40	50	60	70	80	90	100	110	120	130	140
2.5s	3.5s	4.7s	6.0s	7.8s	9.8s	12.1s	15.0s	18.6s	22.8s	30.6s	43.1s

BRAKING

30mph-0	30mph-0	Dry 50mph-0	Wet 50mph-0	70mph-0	70mph-0
10.0m	20.2m	27.3m	30.9m	53.5m	60.4m

ACCELERATION IN GEAR

20-40	1.8
30-50	2.3
40-60	2.6
50-70	3.1
60-80	3.7
70-90	4.3
80-100	5.1
90-110	6.5
100-120	7.9
110-130	11.2
120-140	18.9

MAX SPEED IN GEAR

AUTO

1. **39mph** 6800rpm
2. **70mph** 6800rpm
3. **107mph** 6800rpm
4. **140mph** 6800rpm
5. **146mph** 5270rpm
6. **Kickdown** no result

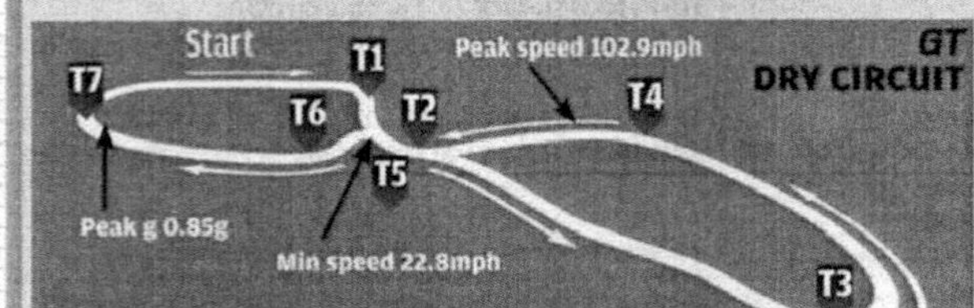

GT DRY CIRCUIT

JAGUAR XK v BENCHMARKS

Jaguar XK	Lap time 1.23.0	**wet patches, bright, 10C**
Aston Martin V8 Vantage	Laptime 1.18.0	**dry and cloudy, 9C**
Porsche Cayman S	Lap time 1.16.9	**greasy, but a dry line, 6C**

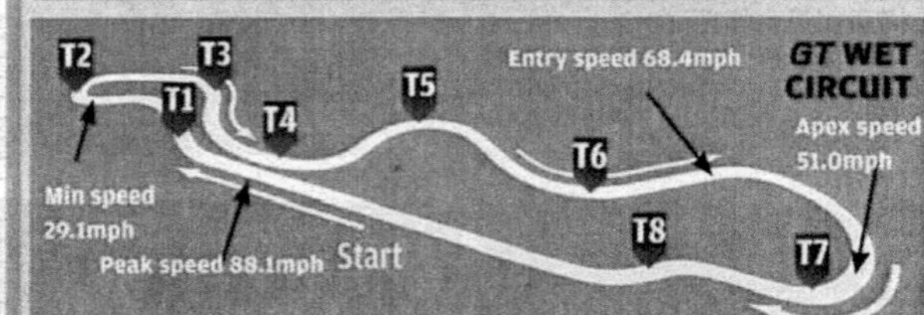

GT WET CIRCUIT

JAGUAR XK v BENCHMARKS

Jaguar XK	Laptime 1.8.3
Aston Martin V8 Vantage	Laptime 1.8.8
Porsche Cayman S	Laptime 1.13.0

Bruntingthorpe drag times

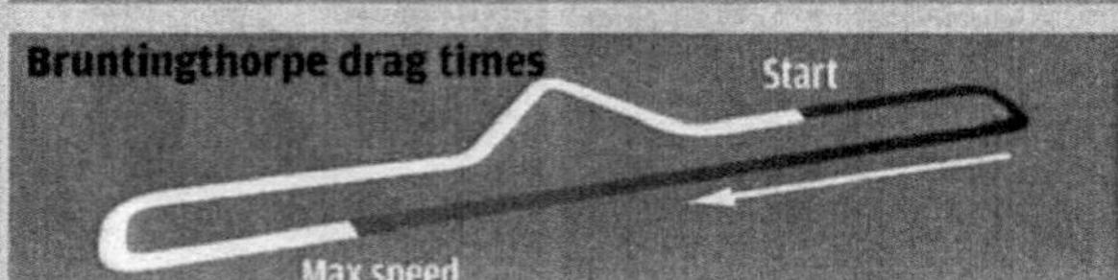

HOW DOES IT COMPARE?

Jaguar XK	146mph
Aston Martin V8 Vantage	165mph
Porsche Cayman S	155mph

ECONOMY

TEST		CLAIMED	
Average	21.9mpg	**Urban**	16.5mpg
Touring	25.3mpg	**Ex-urb**	30.1mpg
Track	10.0mpg	**Comb**	25.0mpg
Tank	71 litres	**Range**	395 miles

CABIN NOISE (Buy it)

Idle 49dbA **Max revs in 3rd** 75dbA
30mph 62dbA **50mph** 64dbA
70mph 68dbA

HEADLIGHTS (Buy it)

Dipped beam Very good
Full beam Very good
Test notes Impressive strength and spread

WIPERS (Buy it)

Preloads wipers with fluid. Effective

TESTER'S NOTES

The Jaguar isn't a circuit car and the lap times reflect that. On the dry circuit it's important to judge the entry speed to corners correctly – especially the long sweeps of T3 and T7 – otherwise the outside front tyre is heavily loaded and the XK understeers. The XK is benign in this situation, though, even with the traction control switched off. Come off the throttle and the front tyres regain grip without any sting in the tail.

There is pronounced body roll through the esses of T2 and the XK feels a little clumsy through the tricky combination of T5-T6. A competent, if slightly uninspiring performance.

On the wet circuit the XK is again very friendly, but it will move to oversteer more readibly.

LATERAL G

Dry na Wet 0.82g

SLALOM

11.6s

Cruiser suspension set-up makes the high-speed slalom tricky. Use the power to steer through

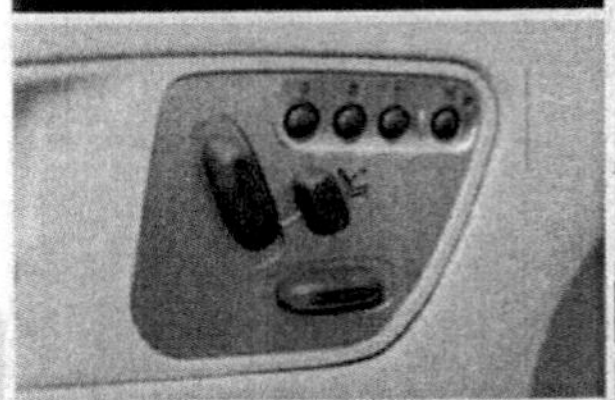

Seat controls on door – makes it easy to see what you're doing

Jewel-effect brake lights attractive, bright

WHAT IT COSTS

JAGUAR XK

On-the-road price	£58,955
Price as tested	£65,934
Retained value 3yrs	na
Typical PCP pcm	na
Contract hire pcm	£1185
Cost per mile	na
CO_2	269g/km
Tax at 22/40% pcm	£377/£685
Insurance/typical quote	19/£721

EQUIPMENT CHECKLIST

Steering reach/rake adjust	■	
Climate control	■	
Automatic gearbox	■	
Electric leather seats	■	
Heated front seats	■	
Satellite navigation	■	
Rain-sensitive wipers	■	
Auto headlamps	■	
Airbags front/side/head	■/■/■	
Anti-lock brakes with EBD	■	
ESP and traction control	■	
Limited-slip differential	na	
Metallic paint	■	
Sport CATS suspension	**£1975**	Buy it
Electric folding mirrors	**£284**	Forget it
Keyless entry	**£430**	Consider it
Rear parking sensors	■	
Xenon headlamps	■	
Tyre pressure sensors	**£400**	Consider it
CD autochanger	■	
Heated front windscreen	**£260**	Consider it
Adaptive cruise control	**£995**	Consider it
Premium Sound System	**£820**	Forget it
18-inch wheels	■	
20-inch Senta wheels	**£2500**	Consider it
Bluetooth compatibility	■	

* Denotes option pack
** As part of option pack
Options in **bold** fitted to test car
■ = Standard na = not available
Buy it / Consider it / Forget it

SEATS
Comfortable chairs offer reasonable support. Nice-quality leather.

WHEEL
Attractive and well-made multi-function wheel works well. Slightly awkward to grip thick rim at quarter to/past mark.

GEARCHANGE
J-gate finally replaced by conventional auto shifter and paddles behind wheel. Both work a treat.

SAT-NAV
New touch-screen system a bit fiddly, layout mostly logical. Plastic surround a rare duff choice of material.

HEATING
No problems here – easy to use and very effective.

CRUISE CONTROL
Radar-controlled cruising works brilliantly; made its debut on previous XK8

most part – very accommodating. That said, the 20-inch wheels our car came on produce a stiff-legged reaction to potholes that the intermediate 19-inch rims largely avoid. But the soothing nature of the XK is what characterises it. Even at a high-speed cruise it remains admirably quiet, only exaggerated road roar on rough surfaces and some question marks over high-speed stability in cross-winds disturbing the calm.

Pick up the pace and the XK subtly responds. It's not a car to pummel the road into submission in order to maintain body control. Instead, the low-speed suppleness persists, even after the CATS system has firmed up the dampers. The XK proceeds as you hoped it might: gracefully and with a pleasingly feline athleticism over challenging roads. The sensation is less raw, less aggressive than you'll feel aboard many of the XK's rivals, but that far from restricts its pace.

The slightly vague 'sneeze factor' remains in the steering around the straight ahead, but once you've turned through that phase resistance builds consistently, and the wheel's general weighting and precision are good. But on a hard drive you'll wish the rack communicated more, that a few layers of numbing assistance would peel away so you felt more connected. This is a car that enjoys rapid but measured progress, rather than being grabbed by the scruff of the neck and driven hard.

The Jaguar doesn't show its claws if you step beyond its limits – understeer is the usual outcome, the absence of a limited-slip differential making it harder to adjust the car's line with the throttle at the limit of grip. That's on a dry road; it's a little easier in the wet.

If the Jag's handling feels slightly benign when pressed, so does the performance. Undemanding driving isn't an issue, but if you suddenly need a burst of acceleration you'll find the V8 wanting. A pedigree GT should accelerate with the kind of authority that doesn't raise doubts, that has the strength to storm effortlessly past sludging traffic. Sadly, the XK doesn't deliver this sensation (though the forthcoming XKR undoubtedly will).

It's not so much the numbers – 0-60mph in 6.0sec and 0-100mph in 15.0 are merely at the head of the hot hatch batch, and considerably slower than a 650i with 5.2sec/12.4sec – but what you feel from behind the wheel. Below 4000rpm the V8 feels flat and restrained. Make the gearbox hang onto a higher gear and the acceleration is subdued enough for you to start willing the car forward.

Rev the V8 out, however, and it brays surprisingly loudly, a note of strain emerging as it closes in on the 6500rpm up-shift point. But the rate of acceleration your ears report doesn't quite tally with what you're feeling. Another 50bhp and an extra 50lb ft of low-rev torque would kill the criticism. Shedding those 130kg would help, too.

We've often praised Jaguar's six-speed automatic gearbox, but it's not without fault here. When you want it to drop a cog with a moderate squash of throttle it remains resolutely in gear, compounding that flat power delivery. Sink your foot further, though, and it suddenly snaps down

TECH JAGUAR XK ALUMINIUM STRUCTURE

JAGUAR'S NEW form of aluminium construction first appeared on the XJ saloon in 2002. Most of the joints are produced using self-piercing rivets applied by hydraulic pressure. Wherever extra strength is needed, an adhesive is used to bond the aluminium together. In fact, Jaguar claims that there is only one weld in the entire fabrication.

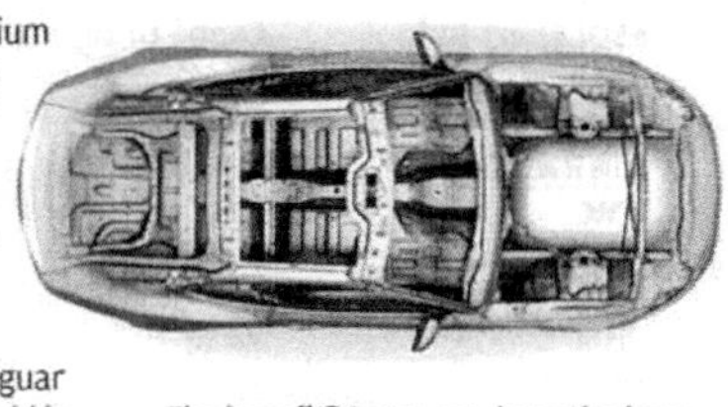

All visible exterior panels are bonded to the underlying structure and there's an automated seam-sealing process to finish it off.

The benefit? Jaguar reckons the long-term durability is twice that of a traditional structure, it's lighter and, thanks to this method of construction, even the convertible doesn't need extra stiffening bars, making it lighter.

a couple of gears and your previously serene advance is interrupted with a jolt and a scream of revs.

That's in 'D'. In 'Sport' mode the gearbox is sometimes too eager to kick down, but partly makes up for this with excellent blipped downshifts that are uncannily well-judged. Manual mode is a sensation for a torque-converter automatic: the shifts are amazingly brisk and there's none of the thump you'd experience with a semi-automatic such as Maserati's Cambiocorsa 'box.

LIVING WITH IT

The XK8's cabin was greatly compromised by using the ancient XJS as its basis. With a fresh start, Jaguar has made amends – at least for the driver. The XK's interior is a world away from its predecessor's, constructed from fine-quality materials for the most part and furnished with a choice of woods or titanium decor that really broaden its appeal. Only some hum-drum plastic cheapens the effect.

The upright dashboard of the XK8 has been replaced by a gently sloping fascia, and it is the better for it. Taller drivers can now get comfortable behind the wheel: there's a good range of wheel and pedal adjustment, and decent head and legroom. It feels more spacious, but remains cocooning, like a good GT should.

Cocooned to the point of entrapment is how you'll feel in the rear – assuming you can get in at all. Even kids will moan, and justifiably. Jaguar defends this with research indicating that's its customers are happy, but that surely doesn't excuse the mediocre 330-litre boot, even if the hatchback makes loading it easy.

One pleasing Jaguar characteristic remains: the XK is good value. Prices start at £58,955, and although this is more than the £55,415 650i, the Jag's excellent standard kit list more than compensates, and never mind the BMW's poor ride and air of relative ordinariness in comparison. More powerful opposition, such as the £66,600 Maserati Coupé GranSport, doesn't offer the wide blend of talents found in the XK, and you'll need £74,125 to drop a V8 in an SL even before options. Despite its drawbacks, no car blends all-round appeal with affordability quite like the Jag.

AUTOCAR VERDICT

The XK's strength lies in the breadth of its repertoire: it both cossets and thrills, depending on mood and situation. This usability is enough to overshadow our disappointment at the XK's final kerbweight and the effect that has on its performance. But all things considered, the XK is easily the best GT all-rounder on sale.

Smooth, svelte all-rounder ★★★★☆

XK only car in the class with a hatchback: makes loading the boot very easy; shame it only offers 330 litres of space

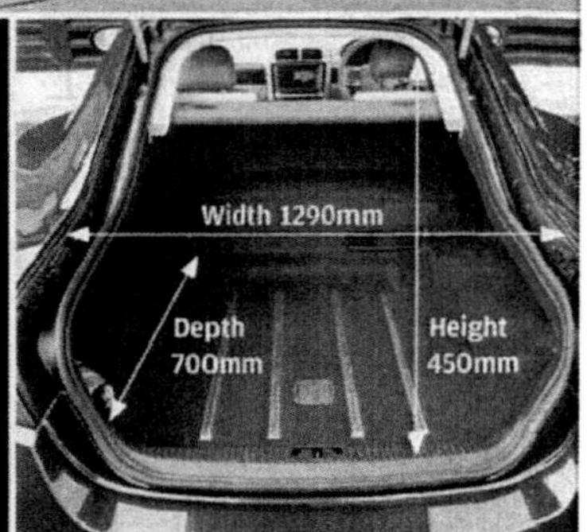

There are two rear seats, but they're virtually useless

INSTANT GROUP TEST Battle of the continent-crushers

	OUR CHOICE 			
MAKE	JAGUAR	BMW	MASERATI	MERCEDES-BENZ
Model	XK	650i Sport auto	Coupé GranSport	SL500
Price	£58,955	£55,415	£66,600	£74,125
Power	295bhp at 6000rpm	367bhp at 6200rpm	395bhp at 7000rpm	381bhp at 6000rpm
Torque	310lb ft at 3500rpm	361lb ft at 3400rpm	333lb ft at 4500rpm	381lb ft at 4100rpm
0-60mph	6.0sec	5.2sec	4.9sec	5.2sec
Top speed	155mph (limited)	155mph (limited)	180mph	155mph (limited)
Fuel consumption	25.0mpg (combined)	25.5mpg (combined)	15.2mpg (combined)	23.2mpg (combined)
Kerbweight	1595kg	1715kg	1680kg	1845kg
Boot space	330 litres	450 litres	315 litres	235/339 litres
CO_2/tax band	269g/km / 35 per cent	286g/km / 35 per cent	434g/km / 35 per cent	291g/km / 35 per cent
We think	A great all-rounder: smooth, svelte and drives, rides and feels good. Ageing V8 engine merely average.	The 6-series has a mighty engine and it's the most practical car here, but it's a rather soulless device.	Brimming with brio and driver appeal; V8 brings genuine supercar sound. Now showing its age in most areas.	Expensive, only two seats and limited luggage space, but otherwise a cracker. Plus you can lower the roof.
VERDICT	★★★★☆	★★★½☆	★★★½☆	★★★★☆

XK is attractive, even muscular from some angles, but conservative overall

Excellent driving position and plenty of space up front; cabin feels special

TEST SCORECARD

ENGINE ★★★☆☆
Charismatic at idle, but showing its age when worked hard. Could really do with more torque at low revs to boost XK's performance.

TRANSMISSION ★★★½☆
Smooth-shifting and quiet, although occasional reluctance to kickdown exaggerates engine's pitfalls. Excellent Sport and manual functions.

STEERING ★★★½☆
Accurate and consistent. Light and easy at low speeds, but doesn't quite weight or sharpen-up enough at high speeds for sporty drivers.

BRAKES ★★★½☆
Slightly numb brakes suitable for smooth stopping – less for press-on driving. Quite easy to get them to fade at the track.

HANDLING ★★★★☆
The XK is a very well-balanced car: it has plenty of grip and a forgiving nature, although there's a surprising amount of body roll.

RIDE ★★★★☆
Much more comfortable than a BMW 6-series in this respect. Decent ride, but optional 20-inch wheels compromised over bumps.

ECONOMY ★★★½☆
Touring figure of 25.3mpg respectable for a 4.2-litre V8. Expect to get over 20mpg in everyday driving. Fair range from 71-litre fuel tank.

DRIVING POSITION & VISIBILITY ★★★★½
XK's cabin far roomier than old XK8's and offers excellent driving position. Visibility is good.

INSTRUMENTS & CONTROLS ★★★★☆
Apart from a few iffy plastics, this is a fine interior. Control are thoughtfully placed and choice of cabin finishes broadens appeal.

EQUIPMENT ★★★★☆
Fine equipment list at the price. Automatic gearbox, electrically adjustable leather seats, sat-nav and xenon lights all standard.

LIVEABILITY ★★★☆☆
On one hand good, as the XK is a very easy car to drive in traffic. However, tiny rear seats and smallish boot count against it.

QUALITY ★★★½☆
XK feels very robust and the detail trim is mostly good quality. Design is mainly excellent.

VALUE ★★★★☆
All things considered, the XK is fine value, although a BMW 650i offers far more pace for less money.

SAFETY ★★★★½
All the airbags you'd expect, a full raft of electronic safety systems, plus a clever, pedestrian-friendly pop-up bonnet.

TRACK WORK ★★☆☆☆
Doesn't feel at home on the track. Soft suspension set-up, it's not that fast and the brakes are prone to fade. Spins an inside wheel easily.

DESIRABILITY ★★★★☆
The new XK is a glamorous car, but we're still not totally convinced that younger buyers will be drawn to it. Nevertheless, it feels special.

NOISE ★★★½☆
Lovely gurgling soundtrack at idle, can sound strained at high revs. Some road noise, but generally very civil.

The 60mph left-hander looked innocuous enough, but for me it summed up what makes Jaguar's new XKR-S so special. We came to it while driving in mid-Wales, not exactly flat out but with commitment, intent on giving the fastest Jaguar since the XJ220 a proper examination on the fine roads near Bala.

The bitumen ribbon rose, twisted and fell almost rhythmically as it speared through wide open spaces, occasionally constrained on the left by barbed wire fences and old stone-block walls. At the end of one of these we arrived at The Bend, a 90-degree left with a disguised apex whose simple purpose has long been to convey traffic around the oblique corner of a field marked by a clump of gnarled wooden posts. The pasture was higher than the road on approach, which fell further as it curved left and out of sight.

We arrived at 70mph, which seemed reasonable given the speed of the rest of the road, but discovered in the last half-second that 50mph would have been a lot more prudent. In an ordinary car, even a decent one, this would have dictated radical action, a big, adrenalin-fuelled armful of left lock, an untidy swerve accompanied by an instant slew of body roll to the right and a couple of yards of road width conceded in reaction time and understeer to put us well and truly into the other lane. It wouldn't have been pretty and might have been dangerous.

But in that instant all of the XKR-S's enhanced abilities came together. I aimed at the apex, ridiculously close. The Jag's quickened steering applied lock with the speed of a boxer's reflexes, yet somehow not too roughly. The wider tyres delivered instant steering authority. The lower centre of gravity and stiffened suspension tamed body roll and weight transfer so there was no lurching. The chassis balance meant that no intrusion was needed from the electronic stability control; the car just turned. The result of all this was that the inside wheels were able to slice through the bend just a couple of feet outward of the apex and we didn't intrude into the oncoming lane at all.

Suddenly, within a second, the steering wheel was straight and the 420bhp, 4.2-litre V8 was gassing rapidly along the next straight. Something deeply impressive had happened, but only one of the car's two occupants (the one whose abilities as a wheelman had been so thoroughly flattered) really knew it.

On the face of it, the XKR-S is a simple proposition: take an already quick and well developed £70,000 coupé, knock off the electronic speed limiter so it'll do 174mph instead of the usual 155, stiffen the suspension, give it bigger brakes and tough-looking black paint, then settle back to enjoy selling the 200 special S-badged versions you're billing as an edition of special driver's cars, knowing they'll sell out in about the 4.9sec it takes the S to sprint from 0-60mph.

There is, however, much more to the XKR-S than that. First, it is the brainchild of two stalwart Jaguar characters – Russ Varney and Mike Cross – whose pooled knowledge on how the fastest Jaguars should drive must surely be greater than anyone else's. Cross is the well known driving guru and keeper of the Jaguar flame whose brief is to maintain 'Jaguarness'; he has the power to sign off every model. Varney is chief programme engineer of the XK range; he has worked on XKs for over 10 years non-stop and knows not just every nut and bolt of the past two models, but all about their owners as well.

Having safely developed the XKR and got it into production, the pair set out to devise, under the radar as it were, the specialist XK they'd build for themselves. Though good, the XKR was intended for all buyers and all markets; this one would be for people who wanted something sharper still, and would understand if they had to compromise a little on ride comfort and road noise. But far from being a routine, beef-everything exercise, the XKR-S project would need to be a collection of subtleties, simply because the XKR already set such a high standard.

For the fastest Jag, which can lay down an easy sub-5.0sec 0-60mph time, the pair decided that the 'standard' 155mph top →

Cabin is all black, including headlining and fascia trim

'S' badging will appear on only 200 hardcore XKRs, and most are already sold; 20-inch, 14-spoke wheels help to lighten the car's unsprung mass

XKR-S has no more power but 155mph limiter has gone

'Despite its stiffer suspension, I think the XKR-S rides just as well as lesser models'

THE POWER OF INDIVIDUALS

How appropriate that the best driver's Jaguar yet should have been created away from the prying eyes of big bosses and bean-counters, as a classic skunkworks project.

Mike Cross (above, left) and Russ Varney (on right) hatched the XKR-S as the kind of XK they'd design for themselves, then sold the management their notion of a batch of 200 premium-priced models. The likelihood must now be that the 'S' suffix will be regularly used in future whenever Jaguar wants to sell the kind of extra-capability, specialist models of which it is so obviously capable.

Jag fans should be delighted with this development. From its earliest days, the company's most iconic models have been conceived by determined individuals, from founder Sir William Lyons (who not only ran the company but also styled the cars) through figures such as Malcolm Sayer, Bill Heynes and 'Lofty' England, to test driver Norman Dewis, who risked the wrath of Lyons by testing prototypes on a Sunday.

Today's Jaguar has iconic figures, too. An obvious one is design director Ian Callum, whose historic achievement has been to discover (and achieve approval for) a much-needed new Jaguar look.

Plug into Varney's huge experience and you begin to understand why the new XK pleases its customers so well; experience the high-speed calm of Cross's driving style and you understand why a Jaguar seems such an effortless drive.
STEVE CROPLEY

Iconic figures have been creating iconic Jaguars since the early days

← speed was rather slow. Varney and his team had run the car at Nardo and in Germany at much higher speeds, so they decided that the XKR-S should be given its head; that meant a 174mph top speed. More engine power would have been nice, but such things entail lots of calibration and clean-exhaust testing, as well as the original modifications, and since it's no secret that there's a 5.0-litre V8 (possibly with direct injection) on the way, mods weren't economic for a 200-car production run.

Higher speeds would need bigger brakes, so the car was kitted with race-bred Alcon six-pot calipers at the front, with four-pot calipers behind. As well as improving ultimate stopping power, these saved unsprung weight (which benefits ride and ultimately roadholding), so the engineers decided to go one step further and use forged alloy wheels that were lighter, even though they were an inch wider.

Which wheels? Not much argument about the need for 20-inchers, either from the designers or the engineers. Pirelli P Zero tyres were adopted, not only because they worked best with the car, but also because Jaguar's people hit it off famously with the Italian firm during the long programme developing the XK saloon.

"The recalibrated springs and CATS adaptable dampers are quite a lot stiffer than a standard XKR, which isn't exactly soft," says Cross. "We tested it and found it worked because the XK body is so stiff and can tolerate it. We took a lot of trouble with actual suspension calibration because this car was never going to be merely a quicker XK. It would be more driver-focused, but it had to become the perfect example of Jaguar's sports car philosophy."

With mass shaved from wheels and brakes, Varney and Cross opted to adjust the tyre sizes too, keeping the 255/35s (optional on the XKR) at the front but progressing to 295/30s (from 285/30s) for the wider rears.

The 14-spoke wheel design is new too. Varney reckoned the S model needed to advertise its toughness a bit, so it was decided that the XKR-S would be built only in Ultimate Black, a deep metallic finish. Jaguar's designers came up with a sophisticated body kit, finished in dark grey, which extends the side sills, lowers the nose a little, surrounds the quad exhausts at the rear and augments the rear spoiler. It also helps the aerodynamics; lift is cut by 60 per cent at the rear and 20 per cent up front, and there's a modest reduction in drag.

The interior is black (or Warm Charcoal) and features a dark Alcantara headlining that definitely adds class. You get a top-level Bowers & Wilkins sound system and a piano black fascia to go with the usual top-level XKR fitments.

You also get the classic XK driving position: hip point not far off the floor so that your legs stretch more out than down, a roomy footwell, a fairly high centre console and a nearly vertical steering wheel positioned so you sit up to it, rather than over it. Your eyeline runs directly over your hands on the wheel, and down the black bonnet with its twin, evocative air outlets. →

'The small increase in steering effort just adds to the car's enhanced sense of purpose'

Jag driving ace Mike Cross admits that some development work was carried out on these Welsh roads; it shows

'The XKR-S glues itself to your chosen line until you do something at the wheel to vary it'

SECRETS OF THE NEXT HOT JAG

XFR will get 5.0-litre, supercharged V8 and more extreme chassis

JAGUAR XFR
SPY SHOT
GAYDON, 21.5.08

The 174mph top speed of the XKR-S gives us a clue that high-performance versions of Jags are getting more hardcore.

When this hot XFR (spied testing in the West Midlands) appears late in 2009, we'll see some of that flavour on the hottest version of Jaguar's stylish four-door.

Power for the XFR will come from a new direct injection, 5.0-litre V8, supercharged to produce 500bhp. Performance will undoubtedly be scorching (think 0-62mph in 4.5sec) and although top speed will be limited to 155mph on standard cars, Gaydon will also offer unlimited, 180mph+ performance as an option.

The hardcore element will come through chassis set-up; the XFR will get a lowered ride height and stiffer springs and dampers than today's sportiest XF, the SV8.

For the first time Jag will have two supercharged engines in a model range when the R is launched, because the SV8 stays in the range as a quick sports saloon.

The SV8's continued presence means that the chassis of the XFR can be tuned to satisfy drivers wanting a more hardcore drive. That differs from previous R models, which have had a compromised chassis retaining a lot of rolling comfort.

Visual subtlety will still be an XFR feature, though. The lower grilles in the front air dam are opened up to flow more cooling air for brakes and dampers and the rear bumper loses the XF's contrasting lower panel in favour of a lower, body-coloured design.

The XFR's quad exhausts will become an R-badge hallmark.

Although this prototype has a body-coloured 'gill' on each front-wing, production versions will have a chromed piece, just like the XJR and XKR. Extra air outlets in the bonnet will improve cooling, and standard 20-inch wheels with the spoke design seen on this prototype will complete the look.

Although Jag has agreed supplies of a new eight-speed ZF auto 'box, at launch the XFR will stick with today's six-speeder. The new eight-speed unit, known as the 8HP, isn't expected in a Jag until 2010/11.

JULIAN RENDELL

Since Cross and Varney were both on hand when we forged into Welshpool (in a standard XKR) to try their new car, the natural thing was to drive with both. Varney is no mean hand at the wheel (which 10-year XK programme boss could afford not to be?) and Cross is a man of unearthly skill. The only part of the day I wasn't really looking forward to was having to drive the pair of them.

Mike began, talking quietly about the XKR-S as he stroked it rapidly across country, managing to demonstrate the upper echelons of its ability while always driving with unimpeachable smoothness. Cross is the world's best advertisement for the school of thought that when you reckon your car needs a performance boost, spend the money on improving your driving.

Surprise number one is just how refined the XKR-S feels. Call me crazy, but despite its considerably stiffer suspension rates, I think it's very little noisier on most surfaces than the lesser models, and that it rides as well. Jaguar doesn't actually claim the XKR-S is as good as the others, but I do. The true test in stiff-suspended cars is how well they cope with suburban ruts and drainhole covers; the XKR-S copes with them brilliantly. The all-aluminium structure resists thumps or echoes very well, and there's a pleasant 'rubber-footed' feel as it crosses the most aggressive-looking craters.

The benefits of the new set-up at the other end of the performance spectrum are obvious. The change in steering gearing is just enough to allow your hands to fall more naturally on the steering in tight, quick going. There's a small increase in effort, partly because of valve changes, partly because of the drag of the slightly wider tyres. It just adds to the car's enhanced overall sense of purpose, as does the 10mm reduction in ride height.

Another spectacular gain is seen in the long, fast bends that abound in Wales. Think about it: cornering at high speed requires inputs so subtle that most chassis/steering combinations simply don't have the precision to keep the car exactly on line. It's here that you learn – in most cars – about the negative effects of lost motion and bump steer. The XKR-S glues itself exactly to your chosen line, despite surface irregularities, until you do something at the steering wheel rim to vary it. The wonder is that it can let you deal out road in centimetres, while never feeling twitchy or over-sensitive.

You pay for it, of course. The UK price is £79,995, and the clear £10k you shell out over the price of an ordinary XKR goes mainly on expertise, exclusivity and subtle suspension tuning, rather than hardware.

XKR-S's role is to blend hardcore with decent refinement

'Think of the XKR-S as a signpost to where the keepers of the Jaguar flame believe it must go'

Nervous? Cropley's far from at ease when chauffeuring Varney, but the XKR-S's chassis helps

Plenty of customers have paid already, though; insiders say most of the cars were ordered after the concept was unveiled at the Geneva show in March.

Is there any point in hyping a car that's sold out? Plenty, actually. Think of the XKR-S as a signpost to where the keepers of the Jaguar flame believe it must go, straight into an area that combines razor precision and huge capability with refinement and driving accessibility. Few can deliver such difficult combinations but the XKR-S shows Jaguar is well advanced with the recipe.

As we drove, Varney enquired whether I reckoned the car's set-up would suit a wider audience (yes to that); he clammed up thereafter, but you can probably conclude that forthcoming 5.0-litre XKRs will draw plenty from this year's S model.

The 200 black XKR-Ss will be built over a fortnight in July, in both left and right-hand drive, for sale mostly in the UK and Germany. The first owners should get their cars in August. They'll soon be driving not only the fastest front-engined production Jaguar ever, but a sure and certain indicator that even greater performance models are not far away. ■

S EXPRESSES

		JAGUAR XKR-S	MASERATI GRANTURISMO S
VITALS	Price	£79,995	£89,000
	0-62mph	5.2sec	4.9sec
	Top speed	174mph	183mph
	Economy	23.0mpg	17.2mpg
	CO_2 emissions	294g/km	387g/km
	Kerb weight	1740kg	1955kg
ENGINE	Engine layout	V8, 4196cc, supercharged, petrol	V8, 4691cc, petrol
	Installation	Front, longitudinal, rear-wheel drive	Front, longitudinal, rear-wheel drive
	Power	420bhp at 6250rpm	433bhp at 7000rpm
	Torque	413lb ft at 4000rpm	361lb ft at 4750rpm
	Power to weight	241bhp per tonne	221bhp per tonne
	Specific output	101bhp per litre	92bhp per litre
	Compression ratio	9.1:1	11.3:1
	Gearbox	6-spd auto	6-spd robotised manual
DIMENSIONS	Length	4791mm	4881mm
	Width	1892mm	1847mm
	Height	1312mm	1353mm
	Wheelbase	2752mm	2942mm
	Fuel tank	70.6 litres	86.0 litres
	Real-world range	357 miles	325 miles
	Boot	300 litres	260 litres
AT EACH CORNER	Front suspension	Double wishbones, coil springs, active dampers, anti-roll bar	Double wishbones, coil springs, gas dampers, anti-roll bar
	Rear suspension	Five-link, coil springs, active dampers, anti-roll bar	Double wishbones, coil springs, gas dampers, anti-roll bar
	Brakes	400mm ventilated discs (f), 350mm ventilated discs (r)	360mm ventilated discs (f), 330mm ventilated discs (r)
	Wheels	9.0Jx20in (f), 10.5Jx20in (r)	8.5Jx20in (f), 10.5Jx20in (r)
	Tyres	255/35 ZR20 (f), 295/30 ZR20 (r), Pirelli P Zero	245/35 R20 (f), 285/35 R20 (r), Pirelli P Zero

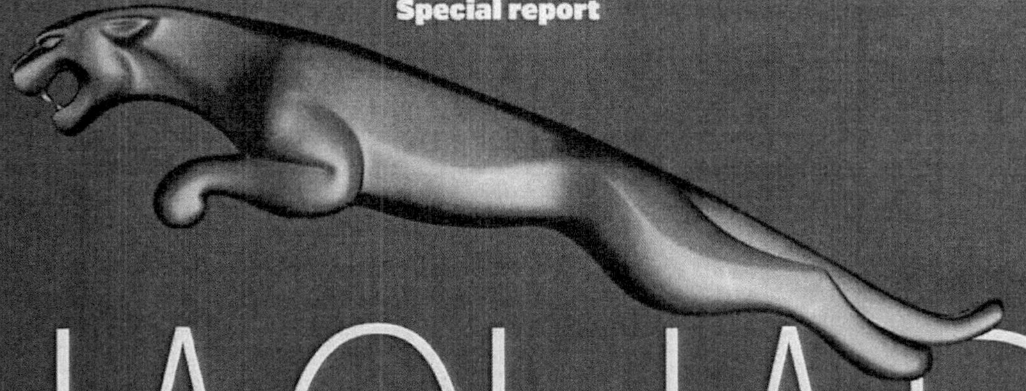

JAGUAR

THE NEXT 10 YEARS

JAGUAR IS coming back. The UK's most famous luxury car maker, bloodied but undaunted by recent strife, has been working on secret, highly imaginative recovery plan designed to restore the marque to its rightful place among the all-time greats of motoring, and to secure its financial footing. As Jaguar's management has already proved, radical action is very much on the agenda, and there is much, much more to come. In this world-exclusive story, *Autocar* publishes key details of Jaguar's planned journey back to greatness.

At a stroke, the new masterplan converts Jaguar into brand of Porsche-like exclusivity, centred on one historically significant but ultra-modern Midlands manufacturing plant, making cars which will be 10 times rarer – yet just as well-built and more affordable – than the best Mercedes and BMW models.

The plan begins with next year's eagerly awaited Jaguar XK grand tourer, the first all-new model from the pen of Jaguar's ace designer Ian Callum. This high-design, old-school muscle car begins a seven-year, non-stop run of remarkable new models designed to restore to Jaguar the unquestioned buyer appeal of its greatest models and greatest days. Now read on.

JAG'S SECRET

Our image shows how 'new E-type' might look: expect it to cost around £30k and go on sale in 2009/'10

MOTOR FORECAST

THE NEW E-COUPE

ALTHOUGH BMW SELLS 3-series models by the boatload, it's the coupé and cabriolet versions that make the healthiest profit margins. Mercedes took the concept a step further and made its C-class-based coupé and cabriolet look like a more expensive model range – and it charges accordingly.

Jaguar's best brains have realised that there's no need to scramble around in the business and leasing end of the pool trying to shift X-type saloons on wafer-thin margins. Replacing the X-type with a compact, 3-series-size coupé or cabrio would lift the marque. The new model would also be easier to sell and serve as an ideal entry point into the brand. Such a car couldn't be based on the expensive corporate aluminium chassis, so Jag needs a good rear-drive platform to build on – and the Mazda RX-8 and new Mustang are the best bets. This car will have to be built abroad – most likely in the US, where the company's substantial female fan base would lap up a compact, sporting Jaguar. And Jaguar would get as close to an E-type replacement as it has ever managed.

FORMULA

- Jaguar 're-booted' as 125,000-a-year marque
- 2005: XJ gets 2.7 V6 diesel
- 2005: Sporty diesel X-type gets punchier engine
- 2006: New XK coupé, rag-top launched
- 2007: 4.0 V8 diesel; 2.7 V6 diesel expands to 3.0 litres
- 2007: Radical new S-type founds new Jag generation
- 2008/'09: Jaguar SUV 'crossover' based on S-type
- 2009/'10: Iconic £30k coupé; recalls E-type era

STORY BY STEVE CROPLEY

Out of adversity, quite often, comes excellence. Despite having been clobbered by every kind of corporate difficulty in the book – from swingeing losses, shrinking exports, the F1 failure and a fraught factory closure to unhelpful public badgering by the country's leading politicians – Jaguar is well advanced with a secret, detailed plan which will re-cast it over the next decade as a small, efficient maker of luxury cars. A Jaguar will become as exclusive as a Porsche, and 10 times more so than a Merc or BMW.

Jaguar's back-room bosses have dumped the idea of expanding production beyond 200,000 cars a year, a basic target of the previous strategy first hatched under Nick Scheele and amplified under Wolfgang Reitzle. They will concentrate instead on maintaining the present production rate of around 125,000 cars, and on making every one of them profitable. The new production rate will be nearly identical to that of super-profitable Porsche, whose success Jaguar would like to emulate. The company believes, and has powerful research to prove, that despite its current travails its image is quite strong enough to sustain the new aims. In fact, the Ford-owned luxury car maker reckons new pitfalls await volume-chasing premium manufacturers in the years ahead, and aims to emerge healthier for avoiding them. Healthier, and with an even better image.

While the new plan gathers momentum and achieves the required approvals (which run through Jaguar's convoluted management structure as far as Bill Ford himself), the company will concentrate hard on enhancing the cars it has. There will be more diesels, and carefully-targeted extra models. Having just turned its best-ever September sales figures, Jaguar believes it can improve things in the short term with careful marketing.

2006: NEW MODEL SPREE BEGINS

Following this consolidation, a new-model spree will begin at the end of next year with the launch of a new XK coupé and convertible – the first all-new model from the pen of Jaguar's eminent design director Ian Callum – and continue in 2007 with a radical new S-type saloon. A year later there'll be a 'crossover' SUV, derived from that car (a near-certain hit in the US, where at least 50 per cent of Jaguars go).

Then, at the end of the decade, the company will unveil a breathtaking new entry-level coupé-saloon to replace the current X-type. The new car, priced below £30,000 on today's prices, is designed both to sweep away the problem Jaguar has earning profits with its relatively low-volume, low-priced X-type saloon, and to satisfy the worldwide clamour for a Jaguar in the iconic mould of the XK120 (1948) and E-type (1961). These were cars that delighted buyers (and shocked the rest of the car world) for more than a ▸

"Jaguar is well advanced. It has a secret, detailed model plan which will re-cast it over the next decade"

Aluminium chassis, based on that for the XJ, will become more widespread

decade with their revolutionary mix of desirability, modernity and low price.

If this new 2010 coupé can achieve the E-type highs of which Jaguar's hard-pressed management dreams, bosses may also expand part of the company's production overseas to another suitable Ford Group plant – perhaps to Mazda Japan or, as BMW and Mercedes have, to the US. By establishing plants in the US, the German firms improved profitability and reduced their exposure to exchange-rate shifts. Such a move would leave Jaguar's British manufacturing arm as a tightly-knit 100,000-a-year business centred on one plant at Castle Bromwich, refurbished for the original S-type's launch in '99 and source of the aluminium panels for the XJ and – soon – XK models. (That move, incidentally, would suggest that the Halewood factory in Liverpool would by then be partly dedicated to the manufacture of next-generation Land Rover Freelanders, and partly to other Ford group models which share with the Freelander the Ford Focus-Mazda 3-Volvo S40/V50 platform.)

If Jaguar gets the new S-type saloon right, the car can single-handedly turn the company's fortunes around

2004-'05: MORE ALUMINIUM CARS, MORE QUALITY

For all its recent difficulties, Jaguar has learned plenty over the past few years. The all-aluminium XJ luxury saloon is the lightest car in its class. The coming XK will be aluminium, too, and models beyond that will be part-aluminium at least, and built with unprecedented emphasis on light weight. Jaguar has been enjoying the plaudits the XJ has won for its agility and low fuel consumption, and believes light weight (plus the recyclability of aluminium) can be distinguishing features for its future cars.

Jaguar has developed another powerful weapon: quality. Even Sir William Lyons never conquered the problem of building his Jaguars well, but under Ford the problem is in recession. Today's models regularly equal or beat

THE NEW S-TYPE

SUCCESSFULLY RE-DEFINING the S-type will, quite simply, turn Jaguar around. There's huge potential in this market. BMW will build around 240,000 5-series this year and Mercedes around 310,000 E-class models. These cars are the real money generators for the premium carmakers.

Last year, the S-type only just managed to bust the 30,000 barrier, so the development potential in this market for Jaguar is huge. It must, therefore, surely weigh on the mind of design chief Ian Callum that he is putting the final touches to a car that could be the most important ever to wear the Jaguar badge.

The big hurdle, of course, is modernising a very British concept. It's tough, but the Range Rover and Mini managed it. Interior styling and quality will be crucial – the American market has baulked at the cabin of the current XJ.

their German and Japanese rivals in JD Power's customer satisfaction and 'things gone wrong' surveys; a powerful boost in the US market. At home, better quality has helped stiffen Jaguars' resale values and remove a showroom obstacle. The company's quality experts, meanwhile, insist that further progress is coming and that all future Jaguars will have the 'very strong rational appeal' for which Coventry always envied the Germans.

2005-'06: MORE DIESELS, BIGGER DIESELS

The XJ saloon, despite good fuel consumption in petrol form, has been conceding company car sales to diesel-powered German luxury cars. It will finally be launched in September next year with the same 2.7-litre, 206bhp twin-turbo diesel V6 diesel recently launched in the S-type. There will be no power difference at first between XJ and S-type diesels but Jaguar sees no problem with that: the S-type has already been praised for refinement and power and, though larger, the XJ is ◆

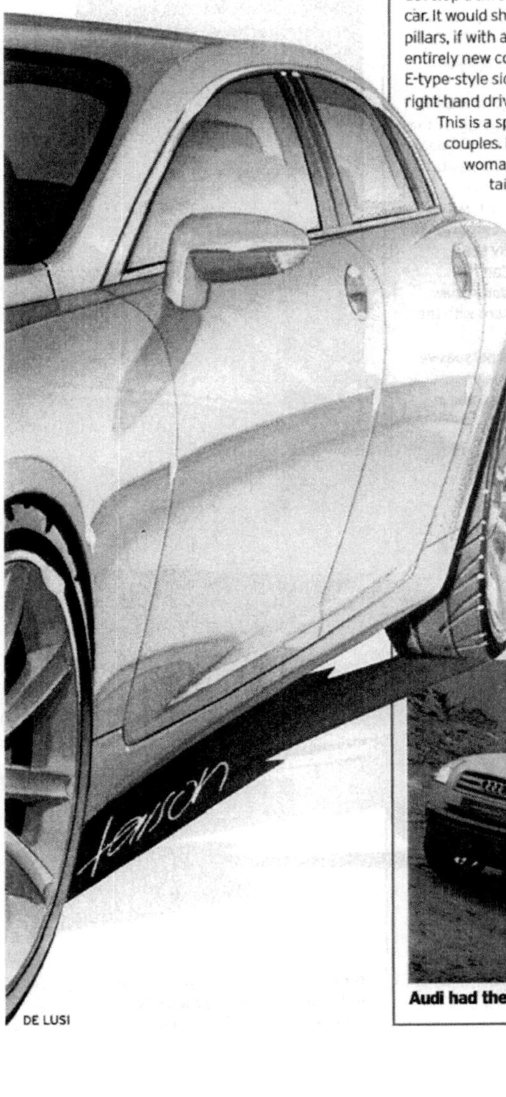

DE LUSI

Our four-point Jaguar fightback plan

Richard Bremner's worked out his own four-part product strategy designed to take Jaguar into a brave new world

PRODUCT PLANNING? THAT'S easy from the comfort of your armchair, your daydreams unencumbered by the financial, industrial and practical impediments that might stand between your fantasy and reality. But never mind that – here's our fearless four-point plan that builds on what we've revealed Jaguar to be doing already.

Okay, he's a journalist, not a product planner. Still, it was fun producing our own plan for Jaguar's evolution

1 RESKIN THE XJ

This is a fine car, all the more so because of its advanced lightweight aluminium body construction. Trouble is, it doesn't look advanced, and it will surely age fast with such a traditional, backwards-looking style. It doesn't just need a facelift – it needs a full reskin and a new interior. The mechanicals and understructure could be carried over unchanged, bar light updating, and we'd give it a new name to mark the break from the past that its fresh, beautiful and original look would represent. Jaguar needs this by 2009. At the latest.

2 EXTEND THE NEW S-TYPE FAMILY

Jaguar already has a crossover S-type-based five-door SUV on the way – but we think it should get radical and develop a three-door, high-style coupé version of the same car. It would share the same body structure up to the 'B' pillars, if with a more aggressive front end, and use an entirely new coupé look at the rear, complete with an E-type-style side-hinged tailgate – handed for left and right-hand drive – and folding rear seats.

This is a sportily glamorous SUV for singles and couples. Picture it on California's Rodeo Drive, a woman-who-shops loading her bags through its tailgate. She'll appreciate the higher load-deck, the electrically folding rear seats, and the lofty driving position that its SUV stance provides. This could be a whole new breed of SUV, one that Audi hinted at a few years back with its Steppenwolf concept. Sophisticated suspension and an aluminium construction should produce quite a wieldy, fun-to-drive 4x4, while its modern, luxury interior – perhaps inspired by the R-D6 concept – would be the finishing flourish for a car that could make Jaguar an innovator again. If some other maker doesn't get there first. Out by 2008.

3 BUILD THE WORLD'S SLEEKEST SEVEN-SEATER

Another crossover SUV, this machine is based on XJ aluminium architecture, and pitched at the top end of the market. Svelte, muscled, sporting but practical, this is your supreme sports-luxury MPV. True, the fold-flat third row of seats may prove impossible to package with the existing XJ rear suspension, but with the appeal of luxury saloons in decline, this car could redefine family luxury wheels, and with the right styling could make a terrific flagship. On sale 2010.

4 WIN THE PERFORMANCE, ECONOMY AND EMISSIONS WAR WITH HYBRIDS AND LIGHTWEIGHT BODIES

Jaguar has already taken the plunge with its rivet-bonded aluminium body structures. Now it needs to cement that advantage by pursuing an aggressive hybrid strategy. Especially since Lexus will be there soon with the RX400H, and Mercedes isn't far behind with the next S-class. Jaguar cannot afford to get left behind all over again, as it did with diesels. First hybrid by 2010.

Getting left behind is something Jaguar has experienced too much of over the past 20 years. But with these suggestions and the plans it already has in place, perhaps it could get ahead again. The fundamental difficulty, of course, is whether Ford dares to find the money to make Jaguar an innovative, vibrant company with a global annual sales potential well above 125,000 cars.

Audi had the right idea with its Steppenwolf concept

The XJ needs a proper reskin to keep it contemporary

Variants of Jaguar's V6 diesel, recently launched in the S-type, will play a key role in other model ranges

actually around 100kg lighter. Meanwhile the X-type, recently launched in an impressive 2.0-litre diesel version, at about the same time, will get the 150bhp, higher-torque 2.2-litre 'Puma' four-cylinder diesel just launched in the Ford Mondeo. The model will be deliberately sold as a sporty car, and Jaguar will add other performance-oriented diesels as time goes on.

During '07, Jaguar will launch an expanded 3.0-litre, 230bhp version of its V6 diesel, to extend the sporty character to its bigger cars. It will also unveil a new modular 4.0 V8 diesel (which would need 270-280bhp to compete with Audi's Tdi V8) to complete a three-tier range of diesels. The expanded oil-burning V6 and V8 will also bring advantage to Land Rover, which uses the same engine 'families' and could do with more torque from its diesels.

2005-'06: NEW XK COUPE, DROP-TOP

Jaguar will use the debut of its first all-new model since design director Ian Callum took over as a rallying call to the traditional marque values of Grace, Space and Pace. Like its predecessor (whose sales continue to surprise) this will be a big, powerful two-plus-two, made in both coupé and drophead forms, but it will share many components with the XJ saloon.

The all-new styling is modern but slightly understated, with a pronounced Coke-bottle hip and a new expression of Jaguar's famous elliptical mouth. Callum & co considered giving the XK a retractable metal canopy like the Mercedes SL (whose price it plans to undercut by about 15 per cent) but ditched the idea because it required too many styling compromises: in essence a flat, raised rear deck. The Jaguar's continues to be low and tapered, but now has a neat electric tonneau under which the retracted hood is stowed.

The all-aluminium new XK is 100 to 200kg lighter than both its predeces-

THE NEW STATION WAGON

HERE IS AN opportunity for Jaguar to be on the front end of a new trend, rather than trailing behind. The launch of the Mercedes R-class (and to a lesser extent the Chrysler Pacifica) has concentrated the minds of other premium carmakers on what appears to be an emerging sector. This intriguing mix of SUV and upmarket estate is a timely move as influential opinion begins to shift strongly against the traditional SUV in many of the world's cities. Paris and Rome have already moved to ban or heavily tax SUVs, for example.

Even as SUVs gradually become public enemy number one, there will still be a need for upmarket, sophisticated family transport. Volvo's XC90 successfully blended off-road looks with an MPV interior. Conceptually, the next move is to tone down the exterior and reduce the overall bulk yet still include seven seats – something that Mercedes has successfully executed with the R-class. Developing this car will also finally allow the Jaguar styling mould to be smashed.

It may be four or five years away, but a seven-seater, estate-style crossover SUV is in the pipeline

Haven't we been here before?

Twenty-five years ago, Jaguar was in deep trouble. Richard Bremner explains how John Egan pulled a few rabbits out of hats

AT THE START of 1980, Jaguar could only paint its new Series III XJ in three colours because of problems with a new acrylic paint plant. Production was less than half what it had been in 1974, sales of the XJS so low as to be barely worth bothering with. Quality was disastrous, a striking workforce had prompted the possibility of transferring all production from Jaguar's Browns Lane factory to the Rover plant at Solihull, and it was leaderless. The spirit, if not the name of the company, wasn't far from extinction.

Egan had the foresight, experience and charisma needed to rescue Jaguar

Back in 1980 Jaguar was part of British Leyland, or BL, as Michael Edwardes, the dynamic South African charged with sorting out this sprawling, nationalised mess, now called the company. Among his many policies was a reversal of the strategy that had attempted to integrate Jaguar into Leyland Cars, a plan resisted both openly and covertly at Browns Lane.

But it was going to take more than guerrilla resistance to save the company, and in April 1980 Edwardes hired John Egan, then with Massey-Ferguson tractors and a former Leyland man (he had co-created Unipart) to lead the company once again. Through Egan, Jaguar was able to take back control of the troublesome new paint plant, and also integrate BL's Castle Bromwich plant – the very factory on which Jaguar's future is founded today – into its operations once production of Triumph TR7 bodies had ended.

Egan also initiated a campaign to improve quality. BL International, responsible for the marketing and sales of Jaguars worldwide, reckoned this was a task of vastly greater priority than developing an eventual replacement for the Series III XJ. Egan also revitalised Jaguar's motorsport programme, a decision that would eventually see it collect the European Touring Car Championship title with Tom Walkinshaw and the XJS, and winning Le Mans with the XJR-9 in 1988.

Equally important was Egan's persuasive way with the demoralised US dealer network, who would visit Browns Lane in 1981 and leave agreeing to take twice as many cars as they had sold the year before. By 1983 Jaguar had achieved a record 15,000 US sales and the Conservative government was pressuring BL to sell off its most healthy divisions – Jaguar and Unipart. Jaguar was sold off in 1984, and another chapter opened that would lead to Ford buying the company.

With the passage of more than 20 years it's easy to forget just how close Jaguar was to calamity. It is nowhere near that now, even if it has serious problems. Its sales in the US remain reasonable, it has got the quality problem licked, it has a factory equipped with top-class vehicle body construction technology and it has a sound plan that promises to make that single Castle Bromwich factory – and the company as a whole – profitable again. The only thing missing is a leader with the remit and visibility of Egan.

By the end of the '70s, XJS sales had become pitiful

Design director Ian Callum is tasked with giving Jaguar the radical look to match its more exclusive image

XK's life these engines will get direct fuel injection, a move to meet tougher exhaust standards. And there are whispers that the upper-echelon engine will expand to around 4.7 litres, further even than Land Rover's new 4.4-litre version for the Discovery and (soon) the Range Rover.

Early on, extra performance variants above the 400bhp XKR versions aren't on the agenda, but Jaguar has experimented with an XKR-R in the past, and could extract as much as 500bhp from a 4.7-litre version. The XK could also serve as the basis for a GT racer of the future: nobody in Coventry believes Jaguar is out of racing forever, and most believe any reappearance will be in sports car racing.

2007-'08: ALL-NEW S-TYPE STARTS ANOTHER GENERATION

In exactly three years' time, Jaguar gets its first chance to show what kind of company it intends to be beyond 2010,

> 'In exactly three years' time, Jaguar gets the chance to show what kind of company it intends to be'

R-D6 concept mixes familiar Jaguar design cues with strikingly modern ones

sor and its opposition in coupé form, and lighter still than all-steel ragtop competitors such as the new BMW 6-series, which need a great deal of heavy body stiffening. For power, the XK begins life with gently improved versions of its normally aspirated 4.2 V8 (300bhp) and supercharged 'R' version (400bhp). Not too long into the

with the launch of its new S-type saloon. Insiders have long acknowledged that this is to be the defining car of a new Jaguar generation, and 'the most rule-changing model since 1968, when we launched the XJ6.'

The car's size is fascinating, not least because, under present plans, it looks like becoming Jaguar's entry-level saloon; the X-type will by then be facing its demise. The car is at the compact end of the BMW 5-series/Mercedes E-class group, and its outline will be that of a coupé-saloon in the Mercedes CLS mould, except that it will be all Jaguar and will adopt themes which started appearing a couple of years ago on Jaguar concept cars. The bob-tailed R-D6 is believed to show what the new model's frontal features will be like, except there's been further work on the grille. The current feeling is that the new S-type will use a modernised 'shield' air intake, with overtones of the Series 1 XJ6 insert, which Callum has always said was his favourite Jaguar grille.

The car will be low, have a front-

engine/rear-drive layout, and probably not be a class-leader for space. But its cabin and boot room will still be generous, because Jaguar will be freed from the first S-type's need to use a platform from the US-built Lincoln LS, whose rear structure is far from space efficient. Jaguar bosses have said in the past that they are still deciding how much of the S-type will be aluminium, but the reality is that it will need an aluminium sub-structure and a close relationship to the XK and XJ to be built economically on the same line as them. The debate is whether the outer panels are steel or not, for pricing reasons.

Jaguar will use the new S-type to reveal a new direction for cabin design. Whereas the new XK puts a modern slant on traditional 'Spitfire wing' dashboard styling, this new saloon uses traditional materials in new ways: new wood and leather textures, a more complex mix of materials and a departure from the plank-across-dash approach.

There is no hint of retro in the new model, but Jaguar's masters are nevertheless showing how faithful they intend to stay to the marque's traditions by launching a new straight-six petrol engine with this car, a re-engineered, UK-manufactured version of Volvo's current 2.9-litre unit, good for 200bhp normally aspirated, and 290bhp with its twin turbochargers. That begs the question of whether the S-type will also use Volvo's five-cylinder, in-line D5 turbodiesel (163bhp); it can fit the same size engine bay, but would need re-engineering for an in-line rather than transverse layout.

20008/'09: JAGUAR 'CROSSOVER' SUV FOR THE USA

Browns Lane has been eyeing the SUV market for several years, especially since Volvo made such a success of its XC90, and has built several secret concept cars. A Jaguar crossover would be a sleeker, more graceful creation than the XC90, but Jaguar would need to develop its own four-wheel-drive transmission. Four-wheel drive is now considered essential for the US's snowy states. The Jag is sure to be a sleek but fairly high and spacious 4x4 estate with three rows of seats, along the lines of Mercedes' R-class.

There's no doubt that Grace, Space and Pace could be provided by such a

'Browns Lane has been eyeing the SUV market for years, especially since Volvo scored with its XC90'

Jaguar plans to make its turn-of-the-decade coupé as iconic as the E-type

THE NEW XK COUPE & ROADSTER

DESPITE BEING THE third-generation Jaguar coupé after the demise of the E-type, the company's upcoming coupé and roadster family has never come near being seen as a replacement for the E-type. The new XK won't either: it will be priced well into sub-supercar territory. That means that sales will be limited – even the mighty Mercedes SL will sell only 30,000 or so globally this year.

Although it will be cheaper than the SL, you could argue that Jaguar could have gently lowered the market position of the XK, possibly selling it in bigger numbers – certainly above the 20,000 units or so that the XK might see in its best year. By contrast, the cheaper Mercedes' CLK will probably shift over 100,000 units this year. So Jaguar might have found a niche somewhere between these two. With a history of value pricing, it could be argued that the car Jaguar really needed is the equivalent of an S-type coupé.

To underline its exclusive image, the next XK coupé will be pitched into sub-supercar territory where sales will be fewer than 20,000

car, or that it could succeed beautifully in the US, but the project has yet to receive the go-ahead from Ford's Ivory Tower. Structure, suspension, engine line-up, interior hardware and styling influences would directly feed off the radical new all- or part-aluminium S-type, which is just another reason the crossover SUV idea is such a good one.

2009/'10: ICONIC NEW COUPE STOPS THE WORLD

For the third model in its brave new line-up, Jaguar plans a compact tour-de-force, a car so profoundly desirable – and so surprisingly affordable – that it could completely recast the company's reputation. It's a tall order, but top designers Callum (Aston DB7) and Julian Thomson (Lotus Elise) are men who could deliver it. Why a coupé? Because Browns Lane has already spent much money proving that a low-volume F-type roadster will only ever be a marginal earner, and that it cannot fight saloons as established and accomplished as the BMW 3-series with fewer resources and win.

There is gathering evidence to suggest that Jaguar's entry-level car for the next decade won't be a saloon at all, but some kind of free-thinking, beautifully styled coupé, brimming with class and performance, which can command a premium for its beauty yet sit in showrooms a little below today's £30,000 barrier. Jaguar product planners already have two target cars on which they might base this model. First is the highly successful Mazda RX-8. Sales of this have already passed 100,000, whereas the Jaguar would be a record-breaking success if it achieved 40,000. The other is the new Ford Mustang (new platform, rear drive, ideal size) which has already been well received, and has an independent rear suspension coming before long.

It's too early to predict exactly how this new Jaguar will look, but insiders have said that the RX-8 based R-D6 coupé, winner of an *Autocar* design award in 2003, is more of a clue to the future than most people recognise. However, the R-D6's 'suicide' rear doors will not feature, because they aren't compatible with the four-seat cabriolet version that Jaguar is also considering.

> 'Jaguar plans a free-thinking, beautifully styled coupé, brimming with class and performance'

R-D6 concept is said to give a big clue to the shape of the coupé's rear

Conventional engines, rather than Mazda's trademark rotary engine, would be used, one confirming clue being that the R-D6 concept was powered by Jaguar's new V6 diesel. Whatever the final product, the fact that Mazda's design boss is Moray Callum, Jag design boss Ian's brother, might be a clue to where the idea for this Mazda-based car came from.

If the R-D6's nose shows the new S-type, we'd like to think its beautiful bob-tail shows the coupé's rear, right down to its side-hinged load-door so reminiscent of the E-type. But with six years to go, there's only one true certainty about this new Jaguar: that we must wait too long for it. ●

An E-type for the 21st century: it's set to be both supremely desirable and surprisingly affordable

Jag's 'new E-type' (left) could be based on Mazda RX-8 (above), but minus the 'suicide' rear doors

Jaguar XK 4.2

The Jaguar XK 4.2 seen here at the Sheraton Hotel in Knightsbridge